# 50 Ways to Throw Away Your Hard-Earned Money Without Really Trying

## Paul Andrew Smith

Copyright © 2020 by Paul Andrew Smith

The right of Paul Andrew Smith to be identified as the author of this book has been asserted by him in accordance with the Copyright, Designs and Patents Act 1988.

All rights reserved. No part of this publication may be reproduced, distributed, or transmitted in any form or by any means, including photocopying, recording, or other electronic or mechanical methods, without the prior written permission of the publisher, except in the case of brief quotations embodied in critical reviews and certain other non-commercial uses permitted by copyright law. For permission requests, write to the copyright owner or publisher.

Acknowledgements

I would like to thank Annabel Venn for bringing this book to life.

# CONTENTS

1. Gym Membership..................................................................1

2. Smoking..............................................................................3

3. Buying Lunch ......................................................................5

4. Giving to Charity When You Are in Debt ............................7

5. Expensive Weddings ..........................................................9

6. Overspending at Christmas .............................................11

7. Car Washes ......................................................................13

8. Books, CDs and DVDs......................................................15

9. Not Taking Advantage of Cashback.................................17

10. Not Redeeming Gift Cards or Vouchers ........................19

11. Buying Bottled Water .....................................................21

12. Buying Travel or 'Fun Size' Items ..................................23

13. Not Utilising Company Benefits ....................................25

14. ATM Cash Machines .......................................................27

15. Subscribing to Magazines..............................................29

16. Entertainment/Nights Out ..............................................31

17. Buying Petrol ..................................................................33

18. Ordering Takeaways and Buying Ready Meals ............35

19. Buying a Daily Coffee ...................................................37

20. Beauty Products and Make-Up .....................................39

21. Clothes That You Don't Wear .......................................41

22. Car Insurance ...............................................................43

23. Unnecessary Insurance.................................................45

24. Playing the Lottery and Gambling.................................47

25. Mobile Phone Usage.....................................................49

26. Parking Fines and Speeding Tickets ............................51

27. Gadgets and Gizmos ....................................................53

28. Foreign Currency and Transaction Fees ......................55

29. Utility Supplies ..............................................................57

30. Energy Efficiency..........................................................59

31. Impulse Buying .............................................................61

32. Holidays .......................................................................63

33. Hobbies........................................................................65

34. Pets ..............................................................................67

**35. Home Maintenance, Improvements and DIY** .................69

**36. Satellite and Cable TV** ......................................71

**37. Children** ..............................................................73

**38. Buying New Instead of Second-Hand Goods** ................75

**39. Brand New Cars** ....................................................77

**40. Food That You Don't Eat** ................................................79

**41. Buying New Technology** ......................................81

**42. Credit Cards and Store Cards** ...........................................83

**43. Bank Accounts** ..................................................................85

**44. Online Courses** .................................................87

**45. Exercise Equipment** ...........................................................89

**46. Petrol Station & Local Convenience Store Shopping** ..91

**47. Mortgages** ........................................................................93

**48. Buying Branded Products** ................................................95

**49. Not Using Loyalty Cards and Discount Codes** .............97

**50. Debt Advice and Consolidation Loans** ..........................99

## INTRODUCTION

Sometimes the simplest way to save money is to not spend it in the first place. Without budgeting and tracking every penny that goes in and out of your account, it's easy not to notice where some of your hard-earned money goes. Whether it's direct debits you have forgotten to cancel or not negotiating when setting up a new contract, this book will highlight some of the areas where you might be throwing away money without even realising, and suggest some simple tips to help you get your spending on track. With a good budget and a hefty dose of self-control, you'll soon find your savings pot looking that bit healthier!

# 1. Gym Membership

With the best intentions of getting fit or losing weight, it is all too easy to get drawn in by fitness marketing and sign up for a gym membership that you are unlikely to actually get any benefit from. A modest, no-frills membership at your local gym or leisure centre will set you back around £20.00 per month. Or you might be taken in with the idea of premium equipment, an Olympic-sized swimming pool and the luxury spa at an exclusive facility, costing closer to £50 a month. After a few weeks, or possibly months, your interest dwindles or your circumstances change, and gym visits become less and less frequent. You might be tied into a contract, or you might just forget to cancel your membership, leaving you paying for a service you aren't even using. If you're not certain you're going to be a regular gym-goer, a membership is unlikely to be worthwhile. If you've never tried the gym, always take advantage of free gym passes and free trials before committing to a full membership.

Alternatively, there are hundreds of thousands of free online classes, both pre-recorded and live, so you can work out in your living room or garden without having to spend a single penny. For those who prefer being outside, walking and running are free activities that require little more than a decent pair of trainers. Your local park or outdoor area might even have a free outdoor gym with a range of exercise equipment for use whenever you want. And if nothing else, your dog will always be grateful for an extra walk each day.

## 2. Smoking

There are many reasons to consider giving up smoking; arguably the main one is to improve your lifestyle and protect your health, and the health of those around you. Yet smoking can be just as negative for your bank balance as it can be for your wellbeing. Using an app can help you keep track of how much your daily habit is costing you and for some smokers the results can be alarming. Taking the average cost of a packet of cigarettes as £10.80, for someone who smokes a more modest 5 cigarettes a day, it soon adds up to £18.90 a week, or £82.13 a month. For someone who smokes 40 cigarettes a day, that quickly amounts to £151.20 or £657.00 a month – and over 5 years, a whopping £39,420.00!

Some smokers opt for the cheaper alternative of rolling their own cigarettes; a pouch of rolling tobacco and cigarette papers will set you back around £20.00 and whilst you might make a saving compared to pre-rolled cigarettes, it still adds up in very little time. Growing in popularity and cheaper still, is vaping. After an initial outlay for the equipment, the average vaper can easily spend approximately £330 a year on their habit. In any format smoking comes at cost, to both your health and your finances.

## 3. Buying Lunch

If you work in a town or city, it's easy and convenient to pop out each day at lunchtime to buy food from the supermarket or local deli. That tempting £3.50 deal for a sandwich, snack and a drink might look like a terrific deal but have it every day and you'd be spending £17.50 a week, or £822.50 a year. A more premium £7 daily lunch amounts to £1,645 a year. Similarly, if your workspace has a canteen and you have a hot meal or a salad every day, you may not even notice the money slowly disappearing.

It's much cheaper to make your own lunch, be it a sandwich or salad, or leftovers from your meal the evening before. If you don't have time to prepare lunch in the morning before work, consider doing it the night before to save time. You could also take some basic items to work at the beginning of the week, knowing you have something in the office fridge to last you for the duration of the week. Another added health bonus of preparing your own lunch is that you can track exactly what goes into your food – some pre-packaged products can be laced with preservatives, salt and sugar. Savings for your pocket and your health can never be a bad thing!

# 4. Giving to Charity When You Are in Debt

Thousands of charitable organisations are doing hugely worthwhile work to support important causes, from nature, animals, and the arts, through to education, health and crisis-services. There is no shortage of charities asking for your support and as a nation of altruistic givers, most of us are inclined to help others in need. As the saying goes, 'charity begins at home,' and this is true when considering your own situation – you might feel compelled into giving a monthly donation, but if you are in debt, this will only add more pressure to your financial situation. Rather than a regular monthly donation, consider a one-off donation instead – however much you can afford, the charity will be able to put it to good use and will be grateful for your support. There are also plenty of other ways of giving to charity without parting with your cash. You could donate your time – volunteering in a charity shop or doing a street collection – or you could donate your skills to assist with administration or management or offering a prize for a fundraising event. Depending on the cause, some charities will be able to receive donations of unwanted items, such as clothing or toys and games. You could also help by signing a petition or joining a march for a cause you are passionate about. Even if you are short on both money and time, a simple show of support for the cause on social media will always be gratefully received. The decision to donate to charity is often driven by emotion – consider your own finances before contributing to others.

## 5. Expensive Weddings

The average cost of a wedding in the UK is around £25,000. Factor in the cost of an engagement ring and typical honeymoon too and that figure rises to over £30,000. With so many elements to consider, including the venue, outfits, catering, entertainment, number of guests, transport and photo/videography, it's easy to see how it all adds up. And what about all those added extras? Professional photo booths, sweet machines and magicians might be fun for some guests, but they will soon have you reaching for your credit card yet again.

More than half of couples turn to their family for financial help. It's no surprise therefore that many couples are choosing a 'DIY wedding' in order to try and keep the costs down. It might be designing and printing their own 'save the date' and invitations, borrowing some fancy-dress items and buying a few disposable cameras, or buying sweets in bulk from the supermarket to leave on the tables. The average cost of photography alone surmounts to over £1,000 – some couples are now opting for a digital only wedding, without the professionally-designed photo albums showcasing their day. Timing is also key – picking a date in July or August, or choosing to have your reception on Saturday, means that venues and suppliers are in high demand and prices are at a premium. You might have dreamt of the big traditional white wedding since you were young, but try not to forget that the most important element is being stood opposite the person you want to spend the rest of your life with, surrounded by those family and friends who love and support you both.

# 6. Overspending at Christmas

With social media a part of our everyday lives, it's easy to be overwhelmed by images and expectations of the 'perfect Christmas.' No matter how hard you try, it's difficult to avoid photos of people's exotic holidays, extravagant presents, tables laden with feasts of luxurious foods and immaculately decorated trees. There's a societal pressure to join in and celebrate the festive season and it can be really hard on your wallet. And it's not just Christmas Day itself – the extravagance can extend over the festive period, from the beginning of December right through to New Year's Eve. There's the pressure to attend the office Christmas party, and then the dinner with that group of friends you haven't seen all year, not to mention the numerous drinks parties, and that's before the family reunions have even started! You might feel the pressure to have a new outfit for each event and combined with expensive meals and drinks, it can leave you feeling out of pocket before the 'big day' has even arrived.

If you can, it's best to try and spread the cost over the year – starting in January, put a little money aside each month so come December, you will have some extra funds to put towards all the extras and it won't leave you feeling as stretched by the end of the month. Remember too that not all quality time spent with family and friends needs to involve lavish celebrations – sometimes a chat over a festive hot chocolate is a lovely time spent with those you love.

## 7. Car Washes

You may have paid a lot of money for your car, so it's understandable that you want to keep it looking shiny and new. For some drivers that means shiny wheel rims clear of mud and dirt, a paint job gleaming under layers of wax and polish and interiors free from dust and debris. Even beyond the aesthetic appeal, it's illegal for cars to have obscured number plates or headlights, so keeping your car clean is essential to keep it on the road.

If your car is your pride and joy, you could be spending more than £100 for a car detail, a clean so professional it will have your car looking and smelling like new again. A full valet is a less expensive option, taking care of both the interior and exterior and costing around £45 for a medium-sized car. If you're looking for ease and convenience, then that comes in the form of an automatic drive through car wash, found on many petrol station forecourts. A full wash and dry costs an average of £7.30. If you have some spare change, you could always consider supporting a charity car handwash. Of course, the cheapest (free) way to clean your car is to do it at home with a sponge, some detergent, a bucket of warm water and some elbow grease!

## 8. Books, CDs and DVDs

A brand-new paperback book costs around £9.00, with a hardback book coming in at around double that price. Of course, you might long for that 'new book smell', with immaculate, unturned pages, but if you are the type of person who reads regularly you'll find you'll be spending a lot on your reading habit. If you have a local library, or even a visiting mobile library, consider borrowing a book instead. Charity shops and car-boot sales are also great places to pick up second-hand books and there are plenty of local book swap schemes to benefit from. And there has been a shift to e-books, made popular by Amazon's Kindle and Rakuten's Kobo e-readers. E-books are available to buy individually at a fraction of the cost of a physical one. There are even monthly subscription services, costing less than the price for one paperback book, providing access to an unlimited number of e-books – perfect for avid bookworms!

Similarly, new television subscription services are increasingly taking over the entertainment market and replacing the need to buy brand new or used DVDs. Amazon Prime, Netflix and NOW TV give you access to thousands of films, series and documentaries, all for under £10 a month. And there's a similar unlimited service for music lovers, with Spotify and Apple Music regularly topping the polls of the best streaming service. Whether you like to get lost in a good novel, binge the latest boxset or listening to music when out and about, it's worth considering online services, for both the positive environmental and financial aspects.

## 9. Not Taking Advantage of Cashback

It might require some research, but there is lots of 'free money' out there if you know where to look! If you regularly shop online, consider using a cashback website – it's a simple process of visiting the website, searching for the retailer and clicking through to their website to make your purchase as usual. You will receive a percentage of cashback for each valid transaction; it could be a few pennies or quite a few pounds. Popular websites include Topcashback, Swagbucks and Quidco.

You may also have a cashback feature with your bank, or through your credit card. Offers are updated regularly so you'll need to activate the ones you think you might use. Pay for the product or service using your debit card and you'll receive a small percentage of cashback on your purchase. What's best is that it is paid directly into your account at the end of each month, giving your bank balance a little boost! Some credit cards may instead have a flat-rate cashback deal, resulting in a small percentage for every individual transaction.

Cashback is also used as an incentive by energy suppliers or mobile phone network providers to encourage new customers. Providing you do the maths to ensure that the deal is worth it in the long-term, you can make some significant savings on contracts and everyday purchases.

# 10. Not Redeeming Gift Cards or Vouchers

Gift cards are a popular Christmas or birthday present, especially for giving to people that you don't know as well or those who are notoriously more difficult to buy for! They are also popular with businesses who want to reward their employees. Yet a staggering estimated £300million is lost each year from unclaimed gift cards, approximately 6% of those issued. This is because many of them have expiry dates, sometimes obvious and sometimes hidden in the small print terms and conditions. The vast majority of gift cards are redeemed within a few months of being issued, but it can be easy to hide them away in a purse or wallet ready to spend later and soon forget about them. Gift cards for an experience day can vary in their expiry date – sometimes the experience must be booked by the expiry date, other times the activity must have actually taken place, so check carefully if you receive a voucher.

Gift cards are also at risk of becoming useless if the retailer goes bust for any reason, the gift cards can become worthless. In some cases, it might be possible to exchange the vouchers with a different retailer, or you may be able to claim back the cost depending on how the gift card was purchased in the first instance. However, with any type of gift card or voucher, the best advice is always to spend it as soon as you receive it to avoid the risk of it being wasted. And if you are looking for a gift for someone else, perhaps cash is the way to go to avoid the potential restrictions of a gift card or voucher.

## 11. Buying Bottled Water

Tap water typically costs less than 1p a litre; bottled water costs an eye-watering 500 times more than that amount. Some research even suggests that the average person spends approximately £25,000 in their lifetime on bottles of water and soft drinks. The simplest way to cut costs is to buy your own refillable bottle and use fresh water from the tap. There is a huge variety of refillable bottles on the market – large or small, lightweight, personalised, ones that filter water and ones that claim to keep your drink cold for up to 12 hours. You won't be short on choice and after an initial investment (and providing you take care of your bottle with some regular cleaning), it will last you for many more outings than a regular plastic bottle will. Free drinking fountains are gradually popping up all over the place, from shopping centres and airports to parks and high streets, meaning it is getting much easier to keep hydrated on the move without having to spend any money. If you are a regular carbonated water consumer, it might be worth considering a kitchen gadget that can add some fizz to your tap water.

And there is a much darker side to the cost of bottled water. In the UK alone, millions of single-use plastic water bottles end up in landfill every single day, or worse, contribute to the ocean pollution that is destroying our marine life. Since so few plastic bottles are actually recycled, not using them in the first place is the only way to improve the situation, both environmentally and economically.

## 12. Buying Travel or 'Fun Size' Items

That last-minute purchase in the airport terminal for a travel-sized bottle of shower gel? It could have cost you around 7 times more for the convenience. Whether it's toothpaste, deodorant, shower gel or sun cream, per millilitre it is almost always cheaper to buy the product from the high street in its full-size equivalent. If you have certain favourite brands that you use, the most economical way is to buy the largest possible size or stockpile when there is an offer on. Should you need a smaller amount, for example when travelling through an airport or just to take away with you for the weekend, you can then decant the product into refillable bottles or pots. Tonnes of full-sized toiletries are discarded at airports each year having fallen foul of the airport security rules, so with some consideration and forward planning you can ensure that you aren't throwing money away too.

And on the subject of saving money, it's not always true that 'good things come in small packages.' A novelty bag of 'fun size' chocolate or a travel-sized packet of biscuits will undoubtedly cost more per item than their regular sized counterpart. Buying from the supermarket and making up smaller portions will always work out a lot cheaper, meaning you have more money to spend on your travels!

# 13. Not Utilising Company Benefits

As an employee of an organisation you are entitled to several core benefits, including a salary, holiday allowance and a workplace pension. Many companies also offer additional perks and benefits, both to entice new employees as well as to incentivise and reward existing ones. Health benefits could include healthcare insurance or dental care plans, complimented by wellness programmes or subsidised gym membership to help employees to keep fit and healthy. A popular benefit is the 'Cycle to Work' scheme, allowing employees to save around 25% on the cost of a new bike for commuting. All these benefits could save you hundreds of pounds a year on memberships or outgoings, so are well worth taking advantage of. Some companies offer subsidised or even free travel in the forms of a company car or a discounted rail season ticket – it's an easy way to save money on your own travel expenses. An employee referral bonus scheme may also be in place in your organisation and whilst this benefit is perhaps more difficult to take advantage of (unless you know the perfect person for a role!), the reward can be quite sizeable.

## 14. ATM Cash Machines

The majority of cash withdrawals are free, but some independent ATMs do charge a fee, usually between £1 – £2 per transaction. If you need to withdraw cash, look for an ATM at a bank branch (it doesn't even have to be your own bank) as these are almost always free of charge. If you have a branch of your bank nearby, a cashier will be able to process a cash withdrawal over the counter at no cost. Another option is to visit a high-street department store or supermarket, many of which offer cashback on payments made with a debit card.

Our use of money has changed over the years with cheques and banker's drafts on the decline and credit and debit cards found in nearly every purse or wallet. We are not carrying nearly as many notes and coins as we used to, with many preferring the ease and convenience of chip and pin or contactless payments on 'plastic'. For those who do their banking online, it's also possible to link your account with your smartphone for even more convenience. Cash payments are growing less popular with customers and businesses alike; some independent high-street stores have already switched to card payment only. Over time, ATMs could become less economically viable and therefore need to charge for the service of withdrawing cash. If you require cash, finding a free ATM won't save you huge amounts, but it will certainly help you on your way.

# 15. Subscribing to Magazines

For some, there is a simple pleasure in flicking through the glossy pages of your favourite magazine: poring over colourful photos, reading articles and reviews from the experts or tackling the sudoku and crossword puzzles. Sign up for a subscription and the magazines regularly arrive at your door, but soon you find it hard to get some time to yourself and before you know it, there's a pile of unread magazines on your coffee table.

As with so many of our entertainment forms, many magazines are turning to an online subscription-based offering, which generally works out significantly cheaper than the print version. You can set them up either directly through your magazine or choice or check out general magazine subscription companies and you could clinch a much better deal.

Some bank accounts come with a free magazine subscription and whilst it may not be worth opening a whole new account, if it comes as an added perk then it's definitely worthwhile taking advantage. If you want to sample a magazine before committing to a subscription, some offer free trials or a limited number of editions at a reduced price. And if you do really want to read that one article, then buying a one-off magazine is still a saving on a whole subscription.

# 16. Entertainment/Nights Out

The temptation of a night out with friends can be hard to resist, especially for city-dwellers who are surrounded by restaurants, bars and clubs. A quick catch up over a pint or a leisurely 3-course meal in a fancy restaurant; whatever the occasion, many people spend at least one night out per week with friends or colleagues. With the average cost of a pint of beer (£3.67) or a large glass of wine (£4.00) steadily increasing, our very British tradition of socialising in the pub is costing us more and more. Sharing the bill between everyone can also mean that you end up footing more than you budgeted for – this happens especially when alcohol is involved and you are expected to pay an equal portion of the bill when you haven't drunk anything.

Beyond food and drink, other popular activities often have a price tag – a cinema ticket or a game at a bowling alley could set you back around £7.00, whilst a theatre ticket is around £27.00 (or closer to £50.00 in London's West End). Partake in these activities regularly and the costs will evidently start creeping up. As an alternative, meet your friends in the park for a walk, or consider inviting them around for an evening of quality time together with homemade pizza and a film.

## 17. Buying Petrol

The price of petrol fluctuates in line with supply and demand, meaning that filling up your car up one day could be a lot cheaper on another. Generally, the fluctuations aren't huge, so you won't be making vast savings each time, but there are a few tips to ensure that your car isn't another asset draining a hole in your pocket.

It's not always possible if you need fuel in a hurry, but do a quick search to find the cheapest petrol or diesel – even a few pence per litre saves you a few pounds and if you're filling up regularly it will certainly save you money in the long run. Don't wait until your fuel tank indicator is illuminated so you need to visit the first petrol station you see. Typically, petrol stations attached to supermarkets tend to cheaper than independent ones. Of course, much depends on how often you are using your car and the length and style of your journeys. Short trips across town could work out cheaper (and quicker!) if you don't get behind the wheel. If you cannot rely on public transport, walking or cycling to commute, look at the option of car sharing with a colleague. When you do have to use your car, a few simple checks can keep it running as efficiently as possible; keeping the tyres well inflated, turning the air-conditioning off at lower speeds and clearing your boot from unnecessary clutter will all help to maximise the performance of your car, thus burning less fuel. Driving techniques can also minimise fuel usage – by accelerating slowly, braking less harshly and considering your position on the road, you'll be driving far more efficiently.

# 18. Ordering Takeaways and Buying Ready Meals

Traditionally the takeaway might have been saved for a Friday night treat, but these days Chinese, Indian, Thai or Italian cuisine has become a stalwart of our modern diets. At an estimated £8.5billion, the food delivery industry is booming. Brits spend an average of £451 per year on takeaways. As lifestyles become more hectic, time-strapped individuals and families are increasingly looking for convenience and the introduction of food-ordering apps mean it has never been easier to order your favourite dish and have it on the table in under an hour. Just Eat, Deliveroo and Uber Eats hold the market share, showcasing restaurants, cafes and even some supermarkets offering quick, convenient delivery to your home or workplace. Sometimes the temptation is hard to resist, and minimum delivery charges can encourage you to buy more food and drink than you really need. The recent shift towards healthier eating has also seen an increase in the variety of cuisines on offer, with vegetarian and vegan restaurants growing in popularity for that weekend takeaway treat.

Depending on the portion size and dish, ready meals can occasionally work out as a cheaper option as buying all the ingredients and making a meal from scratch. However the way to keep any family food budget as low as possible is to buy groceries and store-cupboard essentials in bulk and make a large number of portions – these can then be frozen for convenience, and ensure you always have a cheap, healthy, homemade meal readily available.

## 19. Buying a Daily Coffee

These days, a visit to a coffee shop can be overwhelming. You can be faced with a menu of around 10 different varieties of coffee, fruit or cream-based iced cooler drinks, mochas and hot chocolate and often a huge selection of traditional, herbal and fruit teas. Tea and coffee are considered a staple of British culture and with cafes and coffee shops on every corner of the high street, you are never short on choice. Whether it's an espresso on our way to the train station, a cappuccino before heading into the office, or a good old cup of tea during our afternoon break, we love our hot drinks. But just how much is our daily addiction costing us? The cost of a daily coffee can vary hugely – a takeaway espresso at a popular café chain costs around £1.50, whereas a speciality latte is closer to £3.00 a cup. For those true coffee connoisseurs, there is even a coffee made from the excrement of a rare South American bird, but it will cost you around £30 for an espresso shot… The average person drinks between 600 and 700 cups of coffee a year, with those purchased from coffee shops or cafes costing around £303. The cheapest way to fund your daily coffee habit is to limit yourself to cups made at home or in the office. If you do visit a café, many chains offer a discount if you use your own reusable coffee cup or mug (and that's before the global benefits of reducing waste!).

## 20. Beauty Products and Make-Up

We've all seen the advertisements: women with gleaming, white teeth smiling from behind plump lips, perfectly manicured nails with a glossy topcoat, and soft, silky hair without a strand out of place. Men too have grey hairs covered up with dye, neatly trimmed beards and faces fresh and moisturised. With such high standards portrayed in the media and in the pages of glossy magazines, it's easy to see how in recent years the UK beauty industry has been valued at around £30billion. But is that brand new face moisturiser at £64 a pot really worth the hefty price tag?

Of course, every person has unique skin and what is best for one skin type might not be suitable for another. A higher price point might be justified for a product that contains premium, organically sourced ingredients, but it is often the branding, packaging and celebrity endorsements that drive up the cost of beauty products. There are plenty of ways to save money when it comes to your beauty regime – switching from liquid soap or shower gel to a bar of soap, ditching cotton buds and make-up removal pads for reusable ones and using olive or coconut oil in place of a variety of creams and lotions. Spend slightly more on make-up items you wear more frequently, such as foundation or blusher, but cut back on the bold, statement items of make-up worn less frequently. Some brands are turning to a new trend of forgoing the appeal of pretty packaging and clever marketing, instead focusing on simple, natural products – better for your skin and better for your pocket.

# 21. Clothes That You Don't Wear

How many items of clothing do you have in your wardrobe or drawers that still have their labels attached? Perhaps it was an impulse buy and you haven't yet found the occasion to wear it, or perhaps you considered it a bargain at the time and simply had to buy it? Or, more likely, you ordered it online and either it doesn't fit or it's not really your style, but you never got around to returning it? If that sounds familiar, then you could be like the average person who amasses around 950 items of clothing in their lifetime that they never wear. That equates to approximately £20,000 for woman, while men spend around half that figure at £10,000.

Next time you are considering a new purchase of clothing or accessories, rather than looking at the price tag as a standalone cost, instead look at the potential lifetime use the item might have. A £50 outfit worn once or twice for a wedding works out far more costly than a £80 pair of jeans you will wear again and again. Keep the mantra of 'buy less, buy better' in your mind to help save you money in the long-term. With increased awareness about the personal cost of the 'fast fashion' industry, more people are looking for sustainable and ethical purchases or turning to second-hand items. If you are looking to clear out your wardrobe and recoup some of your lost money, there are plenty of online auction sites or apps that specialise in brand new or second-hand clothing. It's less likely that you'll recover the full amount that you originally paid for the item, but it's better than hanging unworn in your wardrobe for eternity as a 'waste'.

## 22. Car Insurance

Insurance for your car is a legal requirement in the UK. It protects your car in the event of an accident, theft or vandalisation, as well as protecting you if you are at fault for an accident or collision. When your annual policy is coming to an end, you will be offered a renewal quote – providing none of your circumstances have changed and you haven't made a claim in the previous year, occasionally the price will be lower. However, by not shopping around for new quotes you are potentially missing out on making a saving by switching to a new provider. Use comparison websites as well as going direct to insurers to ensure you get the best deal. Beyond the car itself, quotes are affected by several criteria – accurate mileage estimates, how many drivers you have on your policy and points on your licence, even your job title and industry you work in. There are multiple ways to describe a job and providing you are accurate and honest, a change in job title could alter your quote for the better. Having a long no-claims bonus is the easiest way to drive the cost of your policy down, so if you can, pay the extra to ensure it is protected if you do have to make a claim. Some policies have add-on features, including personal injury cover, a courtesy car or breakdown cover. It can be convenient to add these to your policy, but that convenience can cost you more so always check that you can't find them cheaper elsewhere as a standalone service. If you can budget throughout the year, paying for your insurance in one lump sum can be up to 16% cheaper than paying in instalments.

# 23. Unnecessary Insurance

Some insurance policies are a legal requirement; to get a mortgage it's vital to have buildings insurance and you'll need at least third-party insurance cover to legally drive a car in the UK. Other types, such as travel insurance or home contents insurance, are strongly recommended to provide cover in an emergency such as fire, flood or natural disaster. Insurance exists to protect you or your belongings from a deemed risk of something happening, but if that risk is actually quite minor, then you are essentially throwing money away to cover a hypothetical situation. For example, mobile phones or bicycles can sometimes be included within household contents insurance, eliminating the requirement to buy separate policies – although always check the small print to ensure that offers a suitable level of cover for the cost of the item.

Weigh up your options of paying multiple small amounts 'just in case,' versus one larger amount if you do find yourself needing to repair or replace an item. You may even find that cumulatively you end up paying more for insurance than the value of the item itself. As with all insurance policies, never set your policy to auto-renew as by not shopping around you are potentially missing out on a much better deal. If you feel comfortable doing so, you can also haggle the price with companies to see if they can improve their quote.

## 24. Playing the Lottery and Gambling

As they say, 'you've got to be in it, to win it.' But what are the actual chances of winning the lottery? A £2 entry will give you a 1 in 45 million chance of winning the jackpot. With those odds you are more likely to win an Olympic gold medal, become an astronaut or get struck by lightning. Yet it doesn't stop us fantasising about all the things we could do with a significant injection of cash into our bank account. At one point nearly half of the adult population were regularly buying a National lottery ticket, but that figure is slowly declining as people turn to online gambling, including scratch cards, casinos and betting, where the odds of winning are higher. It can be easy to fritter away money; it is important to never play with more than you can afford to lose. At worst, gambling can become an addiction leading to debt and financial worries.

Some lotteries, including the National Lottery, are set up to benefit multiple good causes, meaning that a proportion of your entry fee goes to charity. Along with the potential of winning big cash sums, some might argue that this is reason enough to buy a ticket each week, but there are plenty of other opportunities to give to charity. Beyond entertainment value, and the hugely slim possibility that you might win a prize, playing the lottery is an almost-guaranteed way for your money to waste away with even realising.

## 25. Mobile Phone Usage

Approximately 95% of the population own a mobile phone. Phone manufacturers and network providers are constantly vying for your attention and there is certainly no shortage of choice – contract or pay-as-you-go, Samsung or iPhone, O2 or EE? Up to around a quarter of people continue paying for their contracts even when they have finished. If you received a new phone on a pay-monthly contract then your monthly charge covers both the handset and your tariff – once the cost of the handset has been covered, you are free to switch to a sim-only or pay-as-you-go contract, both of which are very likely to cost less. If you don't switch or upgrade to a new phone you are essentially paying towards a phone you already own outright. Try and negotiate a new deal with your existing provider or shop around to see if you can get a better deal. Your networks may offer a tool to show your average monthly minutes and data usage (or use previous bills) – this will give you an indication of the allowance you need, so don't end up paying for more than you are likely to use. For heavy data users, a spending cap will ensure that you don't have any nasty surprises when your bill arrives. As many contracts are set up with a direct debit, when your contract ends it can be easy to forget to cancel the automatic payments, sometimes leaving people paying for a service they are no longer receiving. If you are happy with your existing phone and are really watching the pennies, a pay-as-you-go option allows you to track exactly how much your calls, minutes and data are costing you.

# 26. Parking Fines and Speeding Tickets

In the UK there are over 70 reasons why you might receive a driving or parking ticket, with parking without a valid ticket or on double yellow lines, driving over the speed limit and violating low-emission zones being amongst the more common offences. Typically, you will receive one of two types of ticket – a Penalty Charge Notices (PCN), issued by council-employed parking attendants, or a Fixed Penalty Notice (FPN). An FPN is generally for more serious violations and issued by traffic wardens employed by the police. Private landowners are also able to issue Parking Charge Notices, usually for infringements in a car park owned or operated by private organisations.

If you receive a penalty charge notice, you have 28 days to pay the fine from the date of issue. You can reduce this by 50% if you pay within 14 days. There are occasions when you might receive a fine and genuinely were not at fault – in this case you have the option to appeal the PCN and in some mitigating circumstances the fine can be completely written off. Of course, the best way to avoid penalties is by driving safely and not bending the rules. If your vehicle has cruise control, set it to the speed limit on motorways or dual carriageways so that you aren't tempted to increase your speed. When parking, check notices or signs for any possible limitations on timings or other rules – it can be tempting to chance it, but when you return to your car to find the dreaded yellow envelope on the windscreen you'll wish you hadn't!

## 27. Gadgets and Gizmos

There is no end to gadgets and gizmos, designed to make life 'easier' for us. Advancing technology and artificial intelligence (AI) has seen a huge increase in the number of electronic items designed to keep us better connected or more efficient in our daily lives. Yet often we are throwing away money simply because we've fallen for a persuasive sales pitch or jumped on the latest trend seen on social media. The temptation of having the newest mobile phone accessory or having the weather read to us by our virtual assistant can quickly see us reaching for the credit card.

And it's not just technology; the kitchen is a haven for gadgets and utensils. Not only do they take up space in your kitchen, if they aren't removed from your cupboards or drawers and used regularly then they aren't proving their value. The hefty electric items include slow cookers, vegetable steamers, mixers and blenders and that chocolate fountain bought last year on a whim. In drawers sit a plethora of peelers, choppers and tools: an egg slicer, a meat hammer, a melon baller or an apple corer – all of which can easily be replaced by using the basic knife, fork or spoon. And just because it's the newest and most expensive gadget, it doesn't necessarily make it the best tool for the job. Before you buy the next 'big thing', ask yourself if it's really essential? Do you really need a new pizza cutter when a knife will do exactly the same job?

# 28. Foreign Currency and Transaction Fees

Airports across the world are never the best places to withdraw money, despite all the convenient currency exchange booths lined up in the departures and arrivals hall. Even with a promise of no commission or transaction fees, the convenience will cost you and on average you'll get around 10% less cash than if you had planned ahead. If the airport is your only option, be sure to check around to get the best consumer rate possible.

Once you are overseas, there are plenty more opportunities where you could be stung financially. Your bank will often add a foreign transaction fee of around 2-3% for converting your payment to the local currency and that could be on top of the fee for paying in a foreign currency in the first place.

Likewise, if you need to withdraw from a foreign ATM, some will charge you a set withdrawal fee or even a percentage of the total amount.

Several online banks specialise in fee free travel debit or credit cards. If you can, opt for some flexibility by travelling with both a Visa and a Mastercard as some ATMs charge for one but not the other. Another option is to use a pre-paid currency card. When making a card payment or withdrawing cash, you might be asked whether you want to pay in the local currency or in pounds sterling. Opting for the local currency is generally better to prevent the foreign bank or store from making the currency conversion. Whatever you decide, some basic research and planning can save you from lots of little fees which soon add up.

## 29. Utility Supplies

Every home requires access to water, gas and electricity in variable amounts and the first and most important step is to ensure that you are on the best energy tariff for your needs. Bills can vary hugely and unlike other industries, customer loyalty counts for little. Many households don't switch suppliers because it feels like too much of a hassle, but by doing this they are potentially spending hundreds of pounds more than they need to.

Rates are constantly changing, so shop around every year. When contracts end, customers are automatically put onto more expensive standard variable tariffs (SVTs), but a simple switch could see a benefit from much lower introductory rates reserved for new customers. To save time and potentially money, use an energy comparison tool to check deals and rates of multiple suppliers at the same time. Once you are in a contract, submit your meter readings regularly to ensure you are accurately paying for what you are using. If you can, opting to pay by direct debit might make you a slight saving with some suppliers. Most providers also offer a 'dual fuel discount' when you have both your electricity and gas supply with them.

Some homes have a prepayment meter installed, more often for houses that have struggled to keep up with energy payments in the past. Energy is paid for by loading payment via a smart card or top up key – whilst they are useful to help with budgeting, the cost comes at a premium and is a more expensive way to pay for energy. Where possible, see if you can make the switch to a standard meter.

## 30. Energy Efficiency

Firing up the oven, turning on the kettle, switching on the TV, running a bath… everyday activities around the home all have a cost. After ensuring that you are on the cheapest energy tariff, there are lots of little tricks you can do to ensure that your bill remains as low as possible. Reducing your energy consumption doesn't require huge lifestyle changes, just a commitment to save on energy where possible.

If you often find yourself reaching for the thermostat to turn up the heating, once you've put an extra jumper on, check whether you can optimise your house for containing warmth. Double-glazed windows, heavy curtains and draft excluders are great for ensuring heat isn't lost unnecessarily, as will keeping your hot water tank insulated. If you have an open fire or log burner, it can be a cheaper option to only need to heat that one room. Washing clothes on a lower temperature and a shorter spin cycle will save on both energy and water (not to mention it's also better for your clothes!) Switch off lights and lamps off when you aren't using them and even better, switch to energy-saving LED bulbs. Likewise turn off electrical items that you aren't using regularly – the average household is typically wasting over £100 a year on energy that is being unnoticeably depleted, known as 'phantom load'. To save water, ensure that taps are turned off fully every time you use them, opt for showers over baths, and use the hose pipe or power washer sparingly. Being conscious of energy-sapping activities will help you to minimise potential wastage, helping both the environment and your bank account.

## 31. Impulse Buying

Impulse purchases are one of the easiest and quickest ways to waste money. With our current consumption culture most of us are all too guilty of giving in to empty purchases, fuelled by peer pressure, influencers or the desire to have the latest trends. On top of that there is the link between psychology and impulse buying; our purchasing habits can be aligned with our emotional behaviour and we buy when we are looking for an uplifting and positive hit. At worst impulse shopping can become an addiction.

Don't go shopping unless you need to; by not stepping foot into a shop or browsing a website, you won't be tempted by 'window shopping'. Visit the supermarket with a shopping list – shopping only when you need it reduces the risk of falling for half price or buy-one-get-one-free offers (not to mention that you are more likely to make impulse buys when you are hungry!) Marketing departments are adept at placing adverts and products right where they know you will be browsing. Cheap, appealing items near the tills? They are deliberately placed there to encourage you to buy. Everyone loves a good deal and we are more likely to buy something if we feel it is great value for money, even when we never had an intention of buying it in the first place. Take a £100 coat with a 75% reduction – the fit or colour might not be perfect, you might not even need it, but it's a steal at only 25% of the RRP so you buy it. Fortunately, most shops offer a returns policy, so if you quickly decide that actually you don't want it after all you can return it for a full or partial refund.

## 32. Holidays

Couples looking for a romantic getaway, families searching for child-friendly accommodation, groups of friends seeking a beach holiday – whether it's an all-inclusive cruise, a luxury safari, a DIY city-break or the adventure of a lifetime, the travel industry has it all on offer. It's easy to be swayed by cheap deals and free upgrades, but always check the details carefully as this is a marketing tool frequently used by travel companies to encourage you to book and sometimes the deals can appear better than they actually are. Whether you are jetting off overseas or having a 'staycation' closer to home, a few simple tips can save you money. Where possible, travelling out of high season will almost certainly slash prices – avoid school holidays and the times around Christmas and Easter for cheaper rates. If you are searching for short or long-haul flights, rumour has it that the best deals can be found on a Tuesday morning, as Monday night is typically when airlines release their new fares and discounts. When it comes to booking accommodation, you will often find the same hotel at different prices so use a comparison site or book direct for the cheapest rates. Some even offer loyalty schemes, earning you discounts on future bookings. If you have your heart set on a particular hotel or activity, check their prices too as you may find a better deal by booking direct. It's advisable to book any holidays or flights on a credit card as that can offer you some additional financial protection if, for example, the airline or holiday company goes bust. Plan and stick to a holiday budget and you'll have a much more enjoyable holiday on all accounts.

## 33. Hobbies

Interests and hobbies are key to help us relax, unwind and take time to do something we really enjoy. But whether we are starting out with a new hobby, or honing our skills to become an expert, it's very easy to get carried away buying kit and equipment and tools. Painting requires paints and brushes and canvases; cycling necessitates a bicycle at the very least; even those that love to read will need books or magazines in some format.

Purchases for your hobby usually present two options: fancy or functional. Do you want something that will get the job done, or are you set on looking the part too? If you are interested in starting a new hobby, try it out before you commit. Attend free trial classes or borrow equipment from a friend before you take the plunge and buy new kit or tools. That will help you decide whether to make larger financial commitments that you might not actually be able to afford.

Sometimes owning all the equipment will give you the identity of a cyclist or a skier; but if you never seem to find or make the time to regularly get out on your bike or head for the mountains, then all the equipment is a bit of a waste. Likewise, if you want to upskill or gain qualifications, it's easy to get carried away spending money on courses and certificates. Depending on the hobby you could try and monetise it – selling homemade crafts or plants, writing film reviews, entering (and winning!) competitions – and it might just make back some of what you've spent on it.

## 34. Pets

In the UK, around 40% of the population own a pet – more than just animals, they are members of our family. Dogs or cats, birds or reptiles, rabbits or guinea-pigs – they mean a lot to us and we love lavishing them with gifts, but does your pet really need another bandana or a novelty Christmas outfit? Pet accessories are big business, especially for our equine, canine or feline friends. In some cases, it is a legal requirement – dogs must wear a collar bearing their owner's name and contact details – but often it is purely an excuse to spend. Cats can benefit from a luxury memory-foam mattress, whilst your dog can look the part in a matching pyjama set. Ranges of exciting edible treats include alcohol-free dog beer and wine, to a carrot birthday cake for your rabbit. These supplement premium, natural or organic pet food, but in reality, your pet isn't actually going to care what they look like, nor are they going to be able to taste the difference between a budget treat and a premium food specifically marketed for their breed. Grooming costs are also not too far removed from the human equivalent, with a full wash, cut and blow dry for a large dog breed costing more than £50. Add to that the costs of vet bills and pet sitting or dog walking if you work away from home (and unlike a lucky few, aren't able to take your best friend to work with you!) and you could be looking at an average spend of around £500 a year. There is no doubt that our pets provide us with companionship, a positive impact on our mental health and unconditional love, but we can pay a dear price for that.

# 35. Home Maintenance, Improvements and DIY

If you are specifically looking to sell your home, some improvements can add value to your house and increase the asking price. Alternatively, maybe you want to knock two rooms together to create more space, or finally get around to adding that conservatory you have always wanted. Regardless of the size of the project, how much you are willing to spend will determine the quality and timescale and it can quickly escalate if you don't keep to your initial budget.

Depending on what you need to do, you can save some money by doing the simpler jobs yourself – painting a new fence, for example, or putting together a cupboard. It's a good idea to learn how to do the basics and have any necessary tools available, either your own or borrowed from a neighbour. There are thousands of videos and how-to guides out there teaching you how to re-wire a plug, hang window blinds or put up a shelf, and it's usually much quicker and cheaper than finding a professional who can help.

That said, simple mistakes can end up being costly to fix – buying the wrong paint that doesn't quite match or not being exact in your measurements can lead to frustration and a need to throw more money at the problem. DIY should be saving you money, not costing you more. There is an element of risk too, especially with more dangerous power tools, so double check you know exactly what you are doing before you start anything new.

## 36. Satellite and Cable TV

As far as entertainment goes in our homes, the television has reigned supreme since it started springing up in houses in the 1950s. From the original grainy black and white screens, to the introduction of 5 different channels, to the wide-screen HDTVs of today, technology advancement is showing no signs of slowing down. So too are the TV production companies, providing us with an unforeseen amount of choice when it comes to deciding what programmes to watch. There are several paid cable and satellite services, with Sky, BT and Virgin Media battling it out in the top spots. Annual contracts cost a fair penny and unless you watch a lot of live sport or regularly watch the newest film releases, it's likely that you aren't getting the most value for your money. If you have a Smart TV with access to the Internet, you can take advantage of free viewing services such as YouTube. There are also numerous rolling-subscription services, including Netflix, Amazon Prime and Apple TV, available at a fraction of the cost. Since subscriptions are monthly rather than annually, it's possible to sign up, binge a series of your favourite programme and then cancel at the end of the month. And if other members of your household also subscribe to the same service, consider a family plan which will usually save you some money. At the bare minimum, watching live TV will cost you the price of a TV licence, with hundreds of free channels to view at the end of your TV remote. By cutting the TV cable, you can cut your bills too.

# 37. Children

It's easy to see why money disappears quickly when you have children about; they grow quickly, change their minds often and love being spoilt. On top of that there is a societal and peer pressure to spend big on expensive birthday parties or Christmas presents. From new outfits to party bags, parents often spend beyond their means to keep their children happy. Children grow out of clothes as quickly as you can buy them. Toys and games follow rapidly changing trends – something that gets played with solidly one week will be flung to the back of the toy cupboard the next. The same can also be said for hobbies and clubs, many of which require costly kit, uniform or membership fees. For a family of 2 adults and 2 children, it can total well over £100 for a day out to the zoo or a theme park. However, if you can get creative and go beyond the popular products and attractions, there are unlimited ways and means to reduce the amount you spend on children. Spend time outdoors, visit the library for books and films; organise a treasure hunt or cook a meal together. If you are heading out for a family meal, various restaurants offer 'kids eat free' deals. Particularly for babies and young children who don't care or know any better, don't waste money on brand new clothes that will be outgrown in a few months, consider buying second-hand or clothes swapping. If you reward children with 'pocket money', encourage them to save up for items they really want. Instilling good financial habits from a young age will serve them well for the rest of their lives.

# 38. Buying New Instead of Second-Hand Goods

There is no denying that we are in a consumer culture, with mass-production happening across the globe; the planet is positively straining under our consumption. Phones, tablets and laptops mean it's never been easier to browse and purchase things we need or want at the touch of a button. And our desire for 'new' comes at more of a cost than just that of our environment. Some brand-new items are quick to lose their value, especially cars, computers and other electronics. With the rapid speed at which technology is developing, it's not long before a brand-new flagship model has been bumped down the list in favour of the next newer, faster or shinier product. Clothing, toys, games and household items are much the same. In a throw-away society, it can be simple to pick up a used and pre-loved item and with any luck, you'll get it at a fraction of the original cost. With technology or white goods, if you want a recent model a refurbished item can be as good as new. Use websites that specialise in second-hand goods such as eBay, Gumtree and Facebook Marketplace (or join local or specialist buying and selling groups on Facebook). Visit car boot sales, flea markets and attend swapping events for the opportunity to pick up a bargain. Better still, do your shopping in charity shops where you can pick up clothing, books and games and furniture. Your money also goes further by providing a donation to good causes. One person's trash is another person's treasure – not only will you save money; you will also be playing a part in helping to reduce waste.

## 39. Brand New Cars

They may offer reliability and that new-car smell, but brand-new cars are notoriously one of the worst culprits for losing their monetary value. Buying on finance may give you the ability and flexibility to get a more expensive car, but can you really afford it and all the associated costs? Faced with an overbearing car salesperson it can be challenging not to give in to a good sales pitch. Don't be swayed by reasonable sounding monthly payments; it all adds up to a considerable annual and overall cost. Leaving the forecourt, from the first mile you drive your car has become a depreciating asset. Add to that the cost of car insurance, tax, MOT, and servicing, plus fuel and maintenance costs, and you could be forking out huge amounts to hit the road. Leasing a vehicle may work out as a cheaper and better option, but you are still essentially borrowing finance to allow you to buy beyond your current means. Buying a car outright is almost always the best way to keep to your budget. On the other hand, buying a car that is significantly older also carries risks – car tax tends to be higher due to emissions and regular maintenance and service is required to keep it on the road. Learning some basic car maintenance skills will enable you to do small jobs yourself.

During the car's warranty period it's recommended to use a franchise dealer for all maintenance and servicing needs, but once the warranty is over it's usually much cheaper to shop around and find an independent garage who can carry out necessary work. Choose a car you can afford and opt for value and practicality over good aesthetics.

## 40. Food That You Don't Eat

Look through your kitchen cupboards and you're almost certain to find tins and packets of food that have been there for some time. From spices to cereals, it could be that you bought an obscure ingredient for a recipe that you only used once, or that you haven't cleared out your cupboards in a long time. If you are regularly having to clear out the fridge shelves with items that are going off, then it's a sign that you are either buying more than you actually need or not using what you already have. Similarly, if you are throwing out unopened products or ones past their best before date then you are contributing to the food waste issue.

Creating a weekly meal plan and a shopping list will help you to stick to buying only what you need. So too will taking note of what your staples are – what do you throw away very rarely? Buy those items in bulk and freeze them so that you have a stock for when you need to use them. Take advantage of buying fresh food that has been reduced in price – if you don't eat it on the day it can be frozen for a later time and providing you do eat it, you will also be doing your bit to help reduce supermarket food waste. If you are sure that you only need a small or certain portion of an item, buying pre-prepared fruits or vegetables can be a good way to reduce potential wastage, but it almost always works out more expensive than buying loose items or in bulk. If you do find you have more than you need, look up specific recipes to use up items. Frozen or tinned food is also a great alternative to buying fresh, giving you much more flexibility with food preparation.

# 41. Buying New Technology

In recent years technology has been advancing at a rapid rate. There are regular and frequent new updates in specifications and features – almost as soon as you have bought one model, a newer one is released with faster speeds, sharper graphics or better features. Look at the details carefully to see whether the hike in price is worth it; often the upgrades are minimal, enhanced by clever marketing to make it sound like you are getting a significantly better product. Salespeople are skilled at finding opportunities to upsell where they can, especially if they are working on commission. It can be hard not to be talked into buying something that is far beyond what you genuinely need! The average lifespan of a decent laptop is around 3-5 years, accounting for moderate daily usage. Brand new, they can cost anything between £200 and upwards of £2,500. Be clear on what you are going to use it for and if you don't really need that 4K display or faster HDD speed, then don't be tempted to spend more. If you are looking for a new laptop because your current one is broken or underperforming, rather than buying new, consider instead repairing or refurbishing. The same applies to new phones and there can be great deals to be found on a model that is one or two generations behind the newest one. If you need a simple phone or one to be used as a spare, opt for a lesser-known brand to make a saving. Once you've bought a laptop or phone, remember to trade in your old device – you'll be helping to reduce waste and at the same time getting a financial contribution to the cost of your new one.

## 42. Credit Cards and Store Cards

Used correctly for borrowing money, a credit card can enable you to spread the cost of larger purchase as well as provide a level of financial protection. However, used carelessly and you could find yourself with a damaged credit score, stung with additional fees and potentially left in debt. Avoid this with some organisation and planning and stay on top of your spending. Without doubt the best way to use a credit card is to pay it off in full each month – avoiding interest charges and late payment fees and demonstrating that you are a reliable borrower of finance. Without monitoring your expenditure, you may exceed your credit limit and be charged for doing so. Keeping a regular eye on your outgoings will help you stay on top of this and if you know that you are nearing the limit then get in touch with your credit provider or bank and they may be able to increase the limit for you. Set up automated standing orders or direct debits to keep on top of due payments. Some credit cards have a monthly or annual fee, usually with additional benefits – if you aren't using these benefits then consider switching to a free card. If you need to move credit around, look for a 0% interest free card to avoid paying for the transfer.

Essentially, a credit card and store cards provide discounts, points and perks for regular shoppers. But you'll also be charged a fair whack of interest if you don't pay off the total each month. Whichever way you use credit, keep on top of your spending and organisation to avoid paying additional charges for the convenience.

## 43. Bank Accounts

Regularly checking your bank account, made easier with online banking and apps, is the best way to keep an eye on both regular payments and any unexpected charges, where you could be throwing away money. The best bank accounts have a higher interest rate and lower overdraft charges. If you pay a monthly or annual fee for a 'packaged account' – one with 'freebie' extras such as insurance or free foreign exchange rates – check whether you are getting use out of all the extras. It's sometimes better value to have a free account and pay for the add-ons separately. If you have been with the same bank or building society for years without switching, you could be missing out on some great deals. Banks compete to win you over, with offers including free insurance, cashback on purchases, a 0% overdraft or even a lump sum of money paid straight into your account. And the best news is that most banks use an automatic switching service to remove all the hassle of re-setting up outgoing payments.

If you'd prefer to keep all your money in one account, some newer banks offer features which categorise your recent spending – at the end of the month you can see what proportion of your purchases was spent on, for example, groceries, transport, household bills or entertainment. If you have a few multiple accounts, there are various apps that will achieve the same thing. Setting up automated payments, standing orders and direct debits are brilliant ways of not only ensuring bills are paid on time, but can assist with regular saving.

## 44. Online Courses

A host of self-taught musicians, artists or novel writers have honed their art through online learning. It can be hard to resist the offer of an online course boasting a huge price reduction. 95% off an online photography course? 1-month free access to a premium membership course on coding? Not only can targeted and canny marketing language make a deal sound far better than it actually is, there are plenty of badly researched and poorly written courses out there which can leave more than just your pocket feeling empty.

Unless you are specifically looking to do the course, it's another whim purchase that will waste your hard-earned money. An impulse purchase could likely leave you losing interest and not completing the relevant material, hence throwing away your money.

Some courses also have a set time period in which to complete the course, easy to forget and resulting in a waste of effort and money. Before parting with your cash, make use of free content posted online by experts, especially if you are new to the subject matter. It could be car maintenance or beekeeping; there are literally thousands of YouTube and Facebook videos where you can pick up tips and skills. For more comprehensive or professional learning, sometimes resulting in certifications or qualifications, the Open University, EdX and LinkedIn are good options and provide a variety of free courses. Your local library or community centre may also offer a host of free learning resources, so there is very rarely a need to pay for online courses.

## 45. Exercise Equipment

Buying new fitness equipment and clothing is the first actionable step in the right direction for anyone wanting to lose weight or get fit. Alternatively, if you are already a dedicated gym-goer, you may be keen to build up to your own home-gym, but the vast majority of people can do a highly effective home workout with very little or no equipment.

Cardio machines, including treadmills, elliptical trainers and rowing machines all have hefty price tags. Despite all the best intentions, that exercise bike you bought in the sale soon doubles up as a clothes horse and the ab cradle becomes nothing more than another trip hazard. Shops are full of water bottles and yoga mats claiming to help you achieve maximum results from your workout. Rather than falling for empty marketing claims, all you really need to get started is a good pair of trainers, preferably fitted properly for your feet and some comfortable workout gear. There are hundreds of thousands of free exercise classes online, both recorded and live, requiring you to use nothing more than your own bodyweight or a few household items – bottles filled with sand can substitute as dumbbells and a cheap skipping rope or the bottom stair can be incorporated into any cardio session. Rather than indulging in the newest fitness tracker, find a free app which can achieve much the same. Fitness does not have to cost the earth. And if you do still really want that rowing machine or static bike, you can almost definitely benefit from other people's mistakes and pick one up second-hand and (quite likely) barely used.

## 46. Petrol Station & Local Convenience Store Shopping

A packet of your favourite crisps or a sneaky chocolate bar – are you ever tempted to pick up a quick snack at the petrol station? Compare the price of the same product in the supermarket and you'll realise the price is significantly higher. As petrol stations don't make significant money on the sale of fuel, they are left little option but to inflate the prices of their other products. The forecourt is notorious for advertising 'must-have' gadgets – wind-up torches, dashboard cameras or designer sunglasses. And where better to get your attention than at the pump, distracting you from the cost of fuel as you fill up. Outside the store you may find seemingly good offers on anti-freeze products, charcoal or car oil – unless you are in urgent need, you are likely to find these much cheaper elsewhere. Once inside you are faced with great deals and offers littered everywhere to encourage you to purchase (and let's not forget the vastly inflated prices for infamous last-minute flower purchases!)

It's a similar story for smaller, local supermarket branches – Tesco Express, Sainsbury's Local or Little Waitrose stores are always more expensive than their larger superstore counterparts, most in part due to increased operating costs. Across a range of popular items, including milk, bread and eggs, you could end up paying around 15% more for the same product and in some cases up to a gargantuan 177%! Convenience always comes at a cost, so don't make a habit of it.

## 47. Mortgages

It's likely to be your single, largest outgoing and a good mortgage may enable you to buy the property of your dreams, but left with a poor offer, high interest rates and unreasonable terms and conditions, you may end up paying through the nose. With house prices steadily increasing, it's becoming more and more challenging to get a foot on the property ladder. As such there has been a rise in the number of ultra-long 30- or 40-year mortgage offers. The bigger the deposit you are able to put down in the first place and the more you can pay off in the short-term, the less you will need to borrow over the long-term which will stand you in good stead for getting a better interest rate. Opting for a fixed-rate mortgage provides a financially secure forecast, allowing you to budget over a set number of years and protecting you from any steep increase in interest rates. However, it does mean that you miss out on the benefits of reduced interest rates if they drop for any reason, and therefore a tracker or variable-interest mortgage could be a better option for you if you are willing to take on the flexible risk.

Regardless of what you opt for, if you don't review your mortgage once your fixed term is up you could end up paying over the odds – make sure you renew the rate or shop around to ensure you are still on the best deal. Before you commit to any mortgage offer, seek out the services of an independent mortgage adviser to ensure that you get the best deal for you and your specific circumstances. As mortgage advisers generally work with multiple lenders, they sometimes have access to better rates.

## 48. Buying Branded Products

From food and clothing, to technology and medication, big brand names are everywhere. The old saying, 'you get what you pay for' might apply in certain cases but doesn't always follow with branded items – a dearer price tag may not mean higher quality. With clothing, some brands are built with sustainability in mind – usually these brands cost a little more and if you can, it's worth spending that for higher quality fabrics and better working conditions for those who make the product. If you are simply paying for a brand that has clever marketing, packaging and celebrity endorsements, it's hardly good value for money.

With grocery and food products, there are generally four categories to choose from: - premium supermarket brands, popular manufacturer's brands, supermarket own brands and their value range equivalents. Often these premium or luxury branded items are produced and packaged in the same factories as their supermarket brand alternatives – the same or similar product packaged and marketed differently. Try taste-testing a few items and see if you can notice any difference. By downshifting to a lower brand level, you can save hundreds of pounds over a year. Another huge mark-up can be found on branded over-the-counter medicines, which can cost up to eight times more than their generic counterparts. A generic packet of ibuprofen, for example, might cost in the region of 25p, whereas a branded packet of the exact same medicine could set you back around £2 – a huge 700% increase!

## 49. Not Using Loyalty Cards and Discount Codes

There are plenty of coupons, vouchers, offers and discount codes out there to save you money on your shopping, both in-store and online. Sometimes it's a huge discount, sometimes it's a few pounds, but you are missing out on free reductions by not taking advantage of these. We've all experienced that moment when you've found the perfect product online, added it to your basket and clicked through to the payment page to discover the price has risen significantly due to seemingly unreasonable shipping or postage costs. Some stores will offer you free postage if you spend over a certain amount; it can be tempting to buy more to increase your basket value – don't do this unless you actually need the additional item and it costs less than the postage. Some brands will offer you a discount and free postage if you sign up to their mailing list (there is always an option to unsubscribe from ongoing communications in the future if you don't want to hear from them again!) There are also web applications that can be added to your browser that will automatically conduct a search for you, providing a code ready to use when you are.

Most major supermarket brands, and many high-street retailers too, run loyalty schemes allowing you to collect points for every pound you spend with them. These can be exchanged for vouchers and discounts on future purchases. With cards in your purse or wallet, on your key fobs or loaded on to your mobile phone via an app, discounts are easily accessible. With a small amount of effort, you can make savings on many of your purchases and the less money you spend the more you can save!

# 50. Debt Advice and Consolidation Loans

Anyone can get into debt, whether it's regular overspending that gets you into difficulty or falling on unexpected hard times. If you have multiple different debts and struggle to keep organised with the repayments, you might consider a debt consolidation loan, a plan to combine all your outstanding debt into one monthly payment. For the convenience of consolidating your debt, these loans tend to involve a higher rate of interest so the total amount payable could end up costing more than if you kept the debts separately. Similarly, any savings made by only having one loan could end up being erased out by the interest charges and fees for the consolidation. The priority with all debts is to keep the costs as low as possible. A secured loan is commonly made against your home and if for any reason you are unable to make the necessary payments, your house could end up be re-possessed.

It can be a scary and lonely place if you find yourself in debt, with feelings of being in a never-ending cycle. Rather than paying for debt advice with what money you do have, there are plenty of advice services and charities out there who can provide free resources and support – Citizens Advice Bureau, the Money Advice Service and charity Step Change are good places to start. Some organisations will even be able to manage payments to multiple creditors on your behalf, reducing the stress and anxiety that being in debt can cause. Whatever your situation, don't find yourself paying more and adding to your debt in an attempt to reduce it – it will only make the whole process of getting out of the red that much longer and arduous.

# SUMMARY

I hope that this book has opened your eyes to ways in which you could be throwing away your hard-earned money. As a summary, here are a few general guidelines to follow as you move forward, to help take what you have learned here and put into practice.

- Create a budget detailing your income and outgoings and log purchases to keep track of where your money is going.
- Cover any necessary expenses first, then pay off any debt and put money aside for savings, then the remainder can be spent on what you want.
- Before making a purchase, wait out and see if you still want or need it the following day.
- Use apps and trackers to help you keep on top of your spending.

- Never buy something just for the sake of buying something – don't buy stuff on sale just because it's on sale.
- To help prevent impulse purchases, work out your hourly income rate and consider how long you will have to work to earn that money back.
- Before committing to any contract, always shop around to see if you can get a better deal.
- Make use of discounts, vouchers, coupons, codes, and loyalty schemes to make savings on everyday purchases.